# YOUR KNOWLEDGE HAS VALUE

- We will publish your bachelor's and
  master's thesis, essays and papers

- Your own eBook and book -
  sold worldwide in all relevant shops

- Earn money with each sale

Upload your text at www.GRIN.com
and publish for free

**Bibliographic information published by the German National Library:**

The German National Library lists this publication in the National Bibliography; detailed bibliographic data are available on the Internet at http://dnb.dnb.de .

This book is copyright material and must not be copied, reproduced, transferred, distributed, leased, licensed or publicly performed or used in any way except as specifically permitted in writing by the publishers, as allowed under the terms and conditions under which it was purchased or as strictly permitted by applicable copyright law. Any unauthorized distribution or use of this text may be a direct infringement of the author s and publisher s rights and those responsible may be liable in law accordingly.

**Imprint:**

Copyright © 2011 GRIN Verlag
Print and binding: Books on Demand GmbH, Norderstedt Germany
ISBN: 9783668632981

**This book at GRIN:**

https://www.grin.com/document/411972

Kaia Smith

# Motivations of Foreign Aid

GRIN Verlag

**GRIN - Your knowledge has value**

Since its foundation in 1998, GRIN has specialized in publishing academic texts by students, college teachers and other academics as e-book and printed book. The website www.grin.com is an ideal platform for presenting term papers, final papers, scientific essays, dissertations and specialist books.

**Visit us on the internet:**

http://www.grin.com/

http://www.facebook.com/grincom

http://www.twitter.com/grin_com

Kaia Smith

## Motivations of Foreign Aid

As individuals, we are quickly and emotionally affected by knowledge of the difficult economic conditions that inhabitants of the developing world must deal with. We may feel relief in knowing that our national governments are making an effort to share their wealth through bilateral aid to these struggling countries; we may also make our own individual efforts to donate our own time and resources to international organizations that specialize in economic development. However, how often does the average citizen question the sincerity of these efforts? Can we trust that our efforts are translated effectively into effective aid once it reaches the receiving country? It seems that there are many complicated and veiled issues behind the simple image that most donor governments and aid organizations project to citizens of the developed world. In other words, although it is commonplace to imagine that aid efforts and good intentions go hand in hand, it may be important to separate these two variables in looking at the result of aid effectiveness or ineffectiveness. In order to look more closely at this issue, I would like to explore the question: What explains the motivation of developed countries in giving financial aid to the Third world? This should give insight on the issue of whether changes need to be made in the ideology, planning and structure of development economics.

*Traditional View of Foreign Aid*

In the literature concerning this question, there are two general points of view. The traditional conception of economic development does not question the sincerely altruistic intentions of donor governments, and especially of international organizations that are heavily involved in economic assistance such as the International Monetary Fund (IMF) and the World Bank. Furthermore, from a classical economic perspective, transferring resources for capital accumulation to which developing countries do not have access because of political or societal externalities is only a way of opening up markets and using all potential resources in order to lead to a greater benefit for all and more equal distribution of resources. Contenders of this view assume reinvestment: "The reason why savings are low in an undeveloped economy relatively to national income is not that the people are poor, but that capitalist profits are low relatively to national income. As the capitalist sector expands, profits grow relatively, and an increasing proportion of national income is re-invested" (Lewis 1954, 30). The larger the number of underdeveloped countries that can rise up the ladder of development, the more opportunities the rest of the world will have to benefit from higher diversification and specialization of products.

In order to strive for the best possible outcomes for developing countries, there is both conditional and non-conditional aid. Conditional aid, such as loans made by the World Bank in conforming to specific development agendas, has specific time limits or controls on how and where aid can be used. According to this first point of view supporting donors' intentions, conditional loans are more beneficial because they force developing countries to adopt better policies and allocate capital efficiently. This also usually means that there will be more monitoring by the donor country to make sure the money is being used appropriately. However, there is also non-conditional aid, such as one-time grants, that do not have such limitations (Mourmouras and Mayer 2004). This kind of aid is beneficial for strong national governments who may have a better idea of where economic aid would be most effective.

However, many that hold this first perspective take account of the potential ineffectiveness of foreign aid. The three main arguments that explain the ineffectiveness of aid until the current era are misallocation of aid (aid is given to actors who are not able to distribute or use aid effectively); misuse (receiving countries have corrupt governments or incapable bureaucratic structures that use the aid for their own interests); and lastly, that GDP is an inadequate measure of growth, i.e. aid helps in a less conspicuous manner than can be measured at the macroeconomic level (Masud and Yontcheva 2005; World Bank 1998). For example, although the Structural Adjustment program of the IMF and World Bank in the late twentieth century failed to positively impact economic development in the Third world, this was due to mistakes and disregard in development policy rather than actual acquisitive goals by the developed world and intentional aims to exploit and thus maintain underdevelopment in the Third world.

One of the main examples supporting the positive transparency of foreign aid is the intensive effort by such economic institutions as the World Bank to restructure the process of economic aid in response to the previous inefficacies. Rather than the overarching, laissez-faire approach to development through Structural Adjustment, which was a failure, the World Bank and IMF have constructed a new strategy that is better tailored to achieving the end result of economic development for all countries. This new plan, the Poverty Reduction Strategy (PRS), takes into account the importance of focusing on country-specific characteristics, allowing for the possibility of government market intervention. This approach also emphasizes sustainability, thus aid efforts are projected to last for longer periods of time and consider more of the context surrounding and affecting a developing country's economic market in order to promote capable institutions and infrastructure (World Bank and IMF 2005). These renewed efforts offer support for the idea that these institutions and involved governments are truly interested in figuring out how to crack the development code in the Third World.

One example of an adaptive strategy is the creation and proliferation of microfinance institutions. Seen as a method of helping countries develop at a more direct and organic level, MFIs allow for flexible, detail-sensitive, and hierarchical development through the accumulation of capital and grassroots lending practices (Munger 2011). Western creation and investment in these institutions may illustrate a determined effort to get capital flowing in these countries in any way possible.

*An Alternative View of Foreign Aid*

However, these modifications to development strategy do not address donors' self-interests nor combatting opportunities for exploitation. They instead underline the need for the receiving countries' governments to be able to distribute aid efficiently. Could this possibly be a way of diverting attention away from a big problem in the ineffectiveness of aid—self-interested intentions by donor governments? This is the second point of view that we will now explore.

According to this side of the argument, foreign aid is just a veiled way of serving the developed world's self-interests. Self-interest refers to a state's desire to bolster its own power relative to other actors in the global economy, even if this means covertly but deliberately creating detrimental conditions for others. As opposed to the classical economic view that holds that capitalism maximizes the benefits for all who participate in the market as long as capital is available, contenders of this side focus more closely on the relationship between capital, profits and the actors and how this can engender greed.

There are multiple examples that support these claims. If we look at trade networks, especially for bilateral aid relationships, it can be shown that "most donors. . . behave in a rather egoistic way: not only those donors who have particular political linkages with . . recipient countries utilise their official development assistance to reinforce such ties, but also all donors [in this particular study by Barthélemy]. . . target their assistance to the most significant trading partners" (Barthélemy 2005). In addition, aid flows are better determined by past links between countries (such as colonialism or beneficial trade relationships) rather than actual levels of need for economic assistance (Dollar and Alesina 2000). Thus, the level of benefits that a developing country can provide to the donor may be a more likely determinant of aid receipt than simply a developing country's urgency of need for aid.

An important idea to consider is that in developing countries, "if a project is funded by foreigners it will typically also be designed by foreigners and implemented by foreigners using foreign equipment procured in foreign markets" (Hancock 1989). All of these connections back to the donor country mean that a great share of the profits being made in the developing country will inevitably return home. The amount allotted to developing countries goes to multiple domains within the donor's economy, including buying their production equipment and salaries to aid workers; this occurs to the extent that almost three-quarters of every dollar spent on economic assistance gets returned to its original economy (Hancock 1989). Not only can aid be recirculated back to its original source, but it can also serve as a profit-generating industry for developed countries and institutions. The interest rates on loans mean that developing countries are paying back more than what they were given, often to the extent that it worsens their economic condition because of increasing levels of debt.

In this sense, one can argue that development strategies and policies are imposed upon receiving countries, when effective policy would normally come from more local work that is done by inhabitants who are experts of their own conditions. Development policy is often formulated by Western policy-makers with little to no experience with the country. It is an interesting paradox that, especially when it comes to conditional aid, strategies are completely determined by such external sources, but little to no time is spent actually working with crucial actors in the receiving country (Munger 2011; Hancock 1989). Is this due to a lack of trust in the capability of individuals from these nations to create their own development strategies with a little help, or is this more intentional so that developed countries have more leverage over the capital accumulation process? This point of view holds that these tactics are, in fact, intentional so as to add to the potential benefit for the donor country and to fortify its predominant role in the global economy.

These connections and processes strengthen the links between elite representatives from all involved actors. Even in the developed countries, economic inequality exists within the national populations. If those who benefit most from profits are the ones with the most leverage when it comes to deciding and implementing development policy, it is not difficult to imagine that the development policies formulated will be maneuvered to reinforce their dominant position in the economic market. Such policies must be framed as being altruistic or else they risk disapproval by developed countries' publics, or when applicable, the loss of access to their donations or taxes (which then profit the elite). Following the arguments made by Andre Frank, foreign aid can be viewed as a way to reinforce the satellite-metropole relationship that is beneficial only to wealthy capitalists. As capitalists search for more and more opportunities to maximize profits, they exploit the resources and populations of foreign countries. Once a close relationship is established with the developing country (through elites and corrupt governments), the metropole uses the country to its disposal; thus, once this contact has been solidified, the country has no possible future for development except for exploitation and continued underdeveloped status (Frank 1973). Through conditionality, lending institutions can assure that aid is being used in ways that are beneficial to them, and through measures such as high interest rates, one can even argue that these countries are being held down in their underdeveloped conditions intentionally. Even multilateral institutions such as the World Bank and the United Nations are intertwined with narrow business interests and advertise development opportunities as lucrative (Hancock 1989).

Furthermore, the importance of looking into these issues comes out when we look at the efforts that donor governments and even international aid institutions make to hide these issues from their publics. For example, documents that illustrate the interconnectedness of capitalist profit seekers and development work "are strictly withheld from the general public, from community groups concerned about the environmental and social impact of the activities of the global lender, and from people in the Third World whose lives are directly affected by those activities" (Hancock 1989, 160). This issue becomes crucial because it allows for an unintentional perpetuation of an exploitative system with help from people lower down on the hierarchical economic ladder in the lending country who may truly have altruistic intentions. For example, an aid worker who is genuinely interested in helping a certain country to develop may be hired to work in that country to administer a specific development program, without knowing that his or her work is a strategic factor in profiting off of the developing country.

It is important to make several distinctions within this argument between multilateral aid (which usually occurs through non-governmental organizations) and bilateral aid. Studies have shown that NGO aid is more effective than bilateral aid because it has a decreased tendency to involve distorting variables of self-interest (Masud and Yontcheva 2005). Also, since these organizations are more specialized rather than national governments who must tie economic interests into a complicated web of political interests, they have better information and resources in order to potentially have a positive impact on development. However, if we look at the non-altruistic actions of NGOs as discussed earlier, we see that these organizations cannot serve as unquestioned authorities of development policy. NGOs may just reinforce national governments' self-interested development policies; studies show that NGOs allocate aid in large part because of concerns for donor funding (Masud and Yontcheva 2005).

Many of these problems are solved through private flows of aid, such as FDI, that are not necessarily determined by governmental conditions. As Dollar and Alesina found in their study, "private flows respond to the rule of law and good economic policy, and are largely indifferent to. . . the strategic considerations that play such an important role in aid allocations"; however, even this relationship is skewed because these private flows tend to go to higher-income developing countries (2000). Thus, because strategic self-interests of larger economic institutions cannot be avoided, it seems that the answer lies in allowing for grassroots-level donation by people not involved in "metropole-satellite" type relations. However, even this prospect gets tricky. For example, we can look at the problems with the recent developments in MFIs. Although this has been increasing in popularity as a way for developing countries to save themselves from further economic catastrophe, it has been shown to not be effective: cultural contexts created by poverty make it difficult for saving to occur because excess money is needed throughout tight-knit communities; intermediaries who may fix this problem complicate the direct relationship of lender and producer; and the distance and profit-seeking behavior of Western institutions that run MFIs make the translation difficult between capital and investment (Munger 2011). If the problem of underdevelopment were simply capital, the results of MFIs would not be so ambiguous; however, they continue to be supported and thus can be seen as a way for the developed world to continue to make profits from Third World populations, this time through high interest rates.

*Conclusion*

We can therefore see the large contrast in the two general points of view behind motivations for development aid. The traditional point of view, arguing that despite sub-optimal outcomes in the realm of economic development, this field is an adaptive one that genuinely seeks to level the playing field for all global actors in order to maximize efficiency and utility. On the other hand, opponents of this view question the details of the processes of development policy formation that point to more strategic and intentional motives behind the scenes of the continued existence of inequality gaps. In both cases, it is clear that the domain of economic development needs a lot of modification and attention, and possibly redefinition of what the term "development" may mean depending on different cultures and contexts.

The preceding literature suggests that there are many questions that remain largely unaddressed in the wider realm of public opinion. Although the traditional point of view offers an idealistic and positive view of the importance of development aid, it does not fit as well into the details of reality in the Third World. It comes to light that because of the increasing number and interconnectedness of externalities in the global economy, the predictions and prescriptions made by followers of classical economics do not take enough detail into account, and create destabilizing outcomes through simple policy in areas outside of the economy in developing countries. One of the problems with traditional conceptions of development policy is that GDP and macroeconomics provide the leading measure of whether a country is developing or not. Harder-to-measure but important impacts such as increased caloric intake, happier or more comfortable lifestyles, or education are not taken into account, even though they may serve as building blocks for eventual development in capital production and accumulation. However, national governments and most international organizations are not concerned with these alternative types of measures. This affects the information spread about the situation of developing countries, and this skewed vision may even affect genuinely altruistic, private flows of aid by individuals who think they are doing the right thing.

Economics should at its foundation be concerned with entire societies and the individuals that make them up, thus a solution could possibly find itself in channeling public opinion within the developed world in order to be informed about the true conditions and contexts of societies in the developing world. If this relationship is distorted by false information about aid interests and allocation, the true altruism that may exist within the economic system is squandered. From the literature, a possible point can be made that isolation of altruistic interests are important for relevant and monitored approaches to helping developing countries; furthermore, NGOs have the potential to be effective relayers of donations because they span across national borders through a single interest and thus have a strong base of resources in order to fight for a certain cause. Thus, when disentangled from the reigns of self-interested national governments and capitalists, NGOs could be more transparent and effective in foreign aid if guided by individuals who are less affected by greed and profit.

**References**

Alesina, Alberto and David Dollar. 2000. "Who Gives Foreign Aid to Whom and Why?" *Journal of Economic Growth* 5 (Jan): 33-63.

Barthélemy, Jean-Claude. 2005. "Bilaterial donor's interst vs. recipients' development motives in aid allocation : do all donors behave the same ?" Paris: Université Paris I Panthéon Sorbonne.

Econtalk. 2011. "Munger on Microfinance, Savings and Poverty." Mike Munger and Russ Roberts. April 18.

Frank, Andre. 1973. "The Development of Underdevelopment." *The Political Economy of Development and Underdevelopment*, Kenneth P. Jameson and Charles K. Wilber. New York: McGraw Hill.

Hancock, Graham. 1992. *Lords of Poverty: the power, prestige and corruption of the international aid business*. New York: Atlantic Monthly Press.

Lewis, W. Arthur. 1954. "Economic development with unlimited supplies of labour." *The Manchester School of Economic and Social Studies,* 12 (May): 139-191.

Masud, Nadia and Boriana Yontcheva. 2005. "Does foreign aid reduce poverty?: empirical evidence from nongovernmental and bilateral aid." IMF Working Paper.

Mourmouras, Alex and Wolfgang Mayer. 2004. "The Political Economy of Conditional and Unconditional Foreign Assistance: Grants Versus Loan Rollovers." IMF Working Paper.

World Bank. 1998. "Rethinking the Money and Ideas of Aid." <http://www.worldbank.org>

World Bank and the International Monetary Fund. 2005. "Synthesis 2005 Review of the PRS Approach: Balancing Accountabilities and Scaling up Results."

# YOUR KNOWLEDGE HAS VALUE

- We will publish your bachelor's and master's thesis, essays and papers

- Your own eBook and book - sold worldwide in all relevant shops

- Earn money with each sale

Upload your text at www.GRIN.com
and publish for free